Your Brain

Written by
Sally Morgan

Contents

Collins

The control centre

Your brain is the control
centre of your body.
It works 24 hours a day,
seven days a week
for the whole of
your life, even when
you're sleeping.

Controls and checks

Your brain controls everything that's going on in your body. It makes lots of checks too, to be certain that all is working properly. It tells you when you're hungry, tired or in pain. It makes sure that you breathe and that your heart keeps pumping. It's also the place where you do all your thinking and store your memories.

Our brain is the most advanced in the animal kingdom. It allows us to do things many other animals can't such as read, write and learn languages.

3

Many cells

Your brain is found inside your head. It's a surprisingly large organ. An adult's brain weighs about 1.4 kilograms. It's very soft and pinky-white on the outside and grey-white inside.

Your brain is made up of billions of cells. Cells are the tiniest part of your body, so small that you can't see them. There are many different types of cell in your body, each designed to do a particular job. For example, there are red blood cells that carry **oxygen** around your body, bone cells that make up your bones, skin cells that form a covering for your body and liver cells make bile, a liquid that helps to break down your food.

nerve cells

There is fat and water in your brain too, but no blood. Instead, your brain is surrounded by **blood vessels**. Blood flows around your body in blood vessels. The blood brings food and oxygen to your brain.

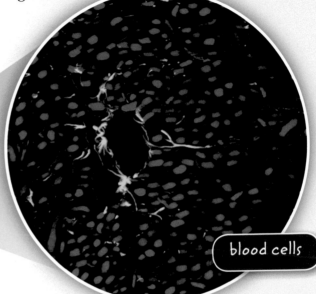

blood cells

Large head

Newborn babies have large heads for their size. This is because they are born with brains that are almost full size. As they get older, their body grows, so their head does not look as large.

5

The three parts of the brain

Your brain is formed from three main parts called the forebrain, midbrain and hindbrain. The largest is your forebrain. Each of the three parts has a different job.

Your forebrain gathers information from your **senses**. This is where you think and where your **memory** is found.

Your midbrain connects your forebrain to your hindbrain.

Your hindbrain is involved with movement and **balance**. It also controls your heart and breathing and helps your **digestion**.

Your spinal cord runs down the middle of your backbone. It carries messages to and from your brain.

Protection

Your brain is protected by the skull. Your skull is a hard case formed from lots of small, flat bones that are joined together. Your brain is also surrounded by three very thin layers of cells, called membranes. These membranes stop your brain from rubbing against your skull. They act as a cushion too, to stop your brain bumping against the inside of your skull when you move or bang your head.

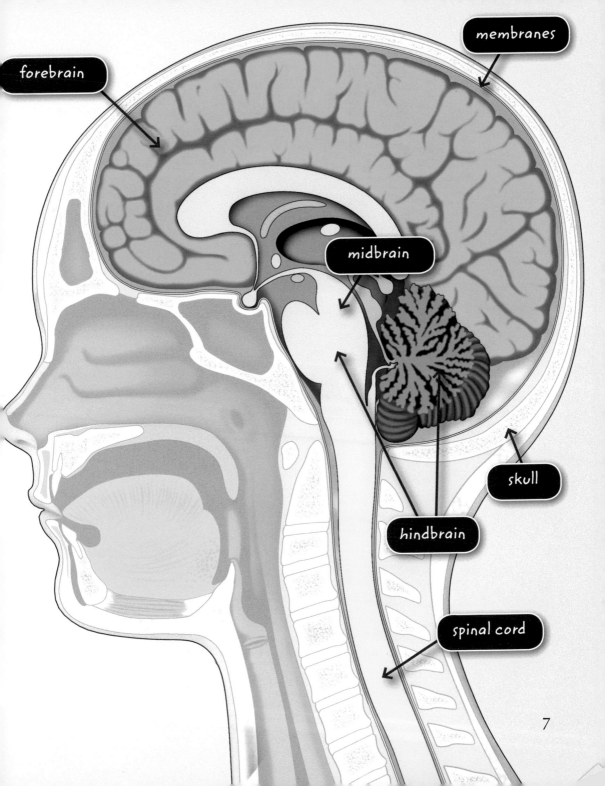

forebrain

membranes

midbrain

skull

hindbrain

spinal cord

7

Networked

Your brain lies at the centre of a huge network
of nerves that runs through your body, from your
toes to the top of your head, and from your
fingers to your heart and lungs.
Together, your brain and nerves make up
your nervous system.

Nerves

Nerves are silvery white, strong
and **stringy**. Inside each nerve is
a bundle of nerve cells.

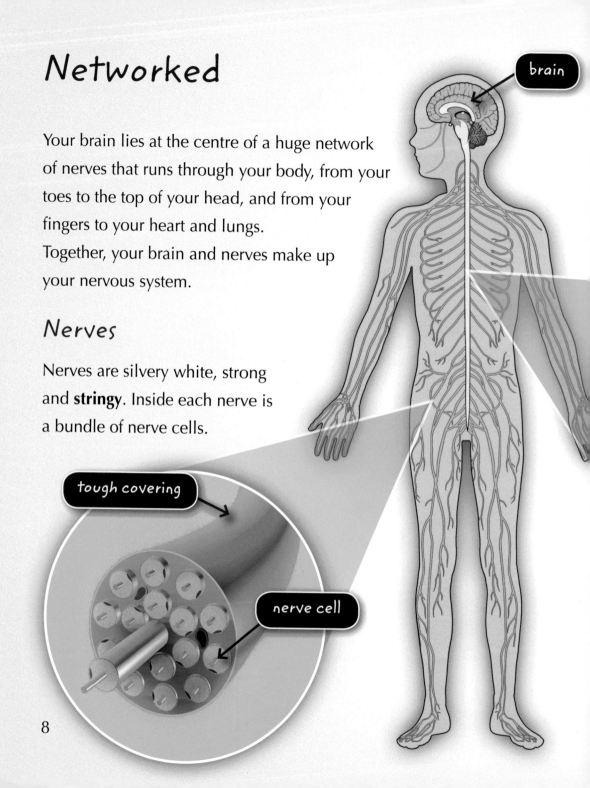

brain

tough covering

nerve cell

The spinal cord

The largest nerve in your body is your spinal cord. It's about as thick as an adult's finger. It connects your brain with the rest of your body. Your spinal cord starts at the base of your brain and extends down the middle of your backbone. Your backbone surrounds and protects your spinal cord from damage. Every second, millions of messages race along your spinal cord, going to and from your brain.

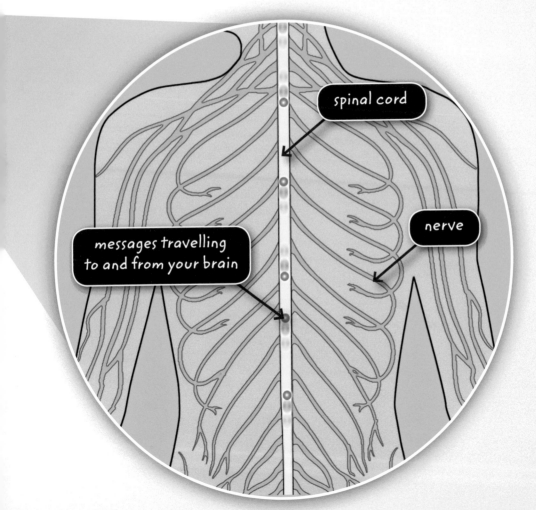

spinal cord

nerve

messages travelling to and from your brain

Nerve cells

A typical nerve cell is made up of two parts.
There is a rounded bit called the cell body,
which contains the general parts of
the cell and the control centre,
and it's attached to
a very long fibre that's a bit
like a wire. The messages
travel along the fibre.
There are tiny branches
coming off the main fibre
that connect to other
nerve cells.

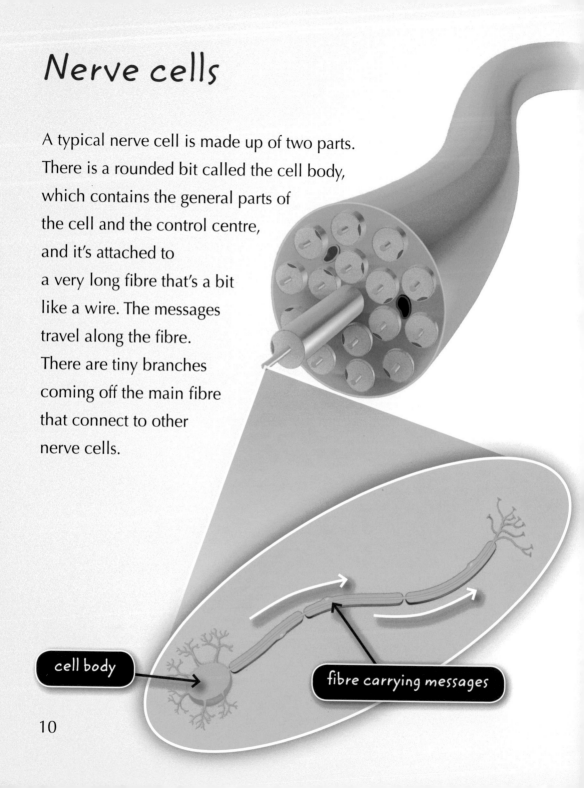

cell body

fibre carrying messages

Some nerve cells are incredibly long and extend to more than one metre in length – for example, the nerve cells that link your fingers and toes to your spinal cord. Many of the nerve cells in your brain are only a few millimetres long or less. They form a network in your brain, linking the different parts.

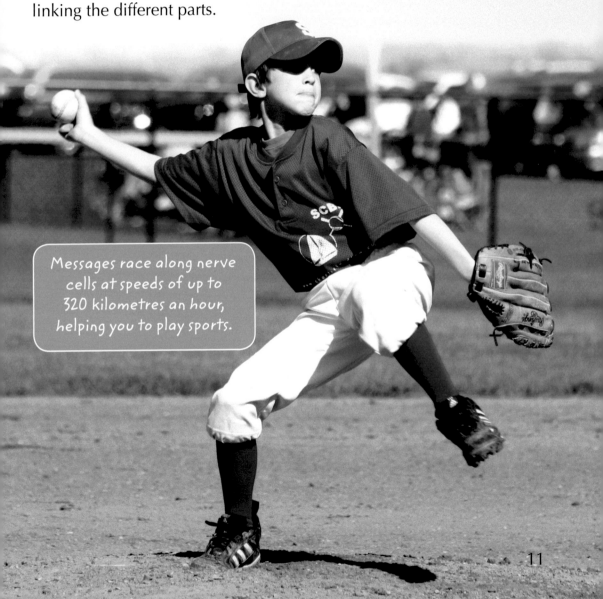

Messages race along nerve cells at speeds of up to 320 kilometres an hour, helping you to play sports.

Connections

Nerve cells have to be connected to each other so that messages can be carried around your body.

Passing the message

A message from your big toe has to travel the length of your body. First, the message passes along a nerve cell in your leg to your spinal cord. There, the message is passed to a nerve cell in your spinal cord, which carries the message to your brain.

The synapse

The place where two nerve cells come together is called a synapse. There are billions of synapses in your body. The two nerve cells do not actually touch but lie very close together. The messages have to jump from one nerve cell to the next.

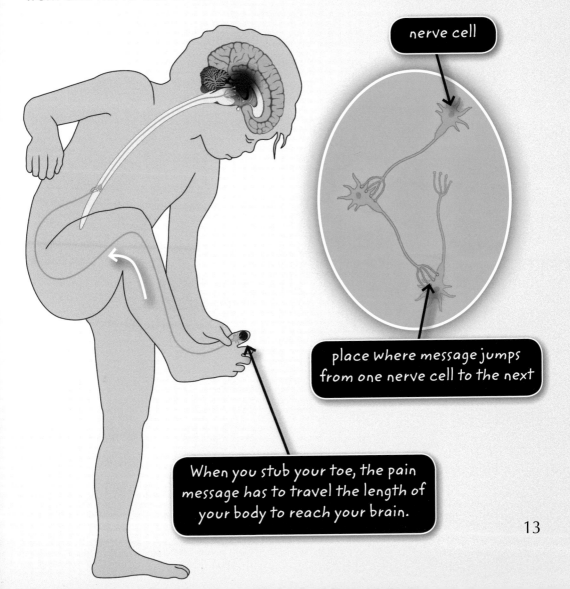

nerve cell

place where message jumps from one nerve cell to the next

When you stub your toe, the pain message has to travel the length of your body to reach your brain.

Carrying messages

Millions of messages pass along nerve cells. The messages carry all sorts of information to your brain, for example information about what's happening outside and inside your body.

Messages leave your brain too. They speed along nerve cells to different parts of your body. They tell the parts of your body what to do and when to move.

From the sense organs

There are two main types of nerve cells. One type of nerve cell carries messages from your sense organs to your central nervous system. These are called sensory nerve cells. They carry information about what you've seen, heard, smelt, tasted and touched. For example, when you hear a sound, a message is carried from your ear to your brain.

fibre

messages

nerve cell endings that connect to other nerve cells

from sense organ or skin

Moving muscles

Motor nerve cells carry messages from your central nervous system to your muscles. When you want to kick a ball, messages race from your eye to your brain. Then the brain sends a message along nerves to muscles in your leg, which kicks the ball.

15

Brain cells

When you're born, you have 100 billion brain cells in your brain. These brain cells stay with you for life. They're the oldest cells in your body.

Never replaced

Your body makes cells all the time. Some of the new cells are used to grow your body, to make you larger and heavier. Others are used to replace cells that have died. For example, red blood cells only live for 120 days so they have to be replaced all the time.

But nerve cells in your brain are different. When you're born, your brain has all its nerve cells in place. Your body cannot make any new brain cells. Once you become an adult, your brain cells start to die and they are never replaced. But don't worry, you have so many brain cells that there are plenty left!

brain cell

Brain connections

Connections are very important in your brain. Without connections you wouldn't be able to think, learn or have memories.

New connections

When you were born, your brain was full of nerve cells, but there weren't many connections. Every time you experienced something new, such as a sound or smell, your brain made new connections.

Remember when you learnt to write. You had to learn how to hold a pen and shape the different letters. Every time you practised writing, messages sped down nerve cells over and over again and your brain made new connections. Once all the connections were made, writing became much easier and you could do it without thinking about it. It was the same when you learnt to run, swim or ride a bike.

Sensing the world

Your brain receives lots of information from your senses. This information is essential to your survival, because without it you wouldn't know what was going on around you.

Five sense organs

Your body has five sense organs – eyes, ears, nose, tongue and skin. Each sense organ is connected to a nerve that carries the sensory information to your brain. For example, your eyes are connected to your brain by your optic nerve.

The first sense to form in an unborn baby is the sense of touc

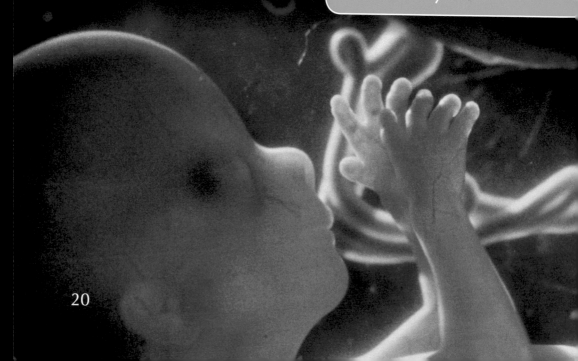

The forebrain

The part of the brain involved with the senses is your forebrain.
This is the largest part of your brain. Its surface is highly folded.
If it was flattened, it would cover two pages of a newspaper.
Within your forebrain are areas that deal with a particular sense.
For example, there is an area that deals with information from
your eyes, while another receives information from your ears.

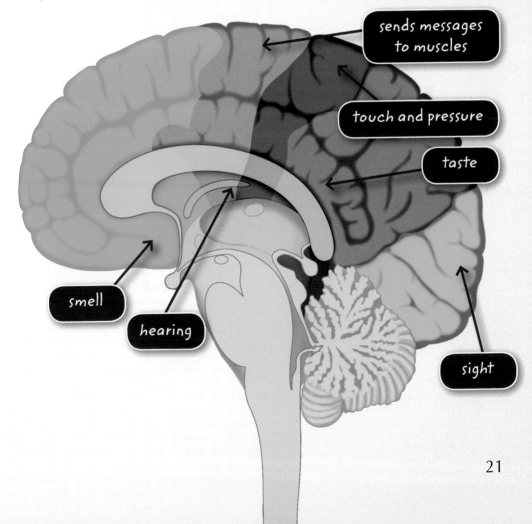

sends messages
to muscles

touch and pressure

taste

smell

hearing

sight

Processing information

Once information from your senses arrives in your brain, it has to be processed. For example, when your brain receives a "picture message" from your eyes, it uses its memories to identify the colours and shapes of the objects in the picture. It processes information from your other sense organs in the same way. When you smell something, your brain searches its memories for that smell so that you can identify it, such as the smell of a perfume or of food cooking.

Making decisions

Then your brain decides what to do with the information. For example, after smelling a plate of food, your brain may decide that it's safe to eat. Sometimes your brain **recognises** an object as being dangerous. For example, your brain tells you that the animal charging towards you is a rhino and you should run away!

Often information is ignored. For example, you can feel your clothes against your skin when you first put them on in the morning. But then your brain ignores the messages from your skin until you think about your clothes. For example, after reading this sentence!

...in from the top you can see that it's split ...n front to back. This forms two halves, ...es.

Rig ...nd left

Generally, the right half of your brain controls the left side of your body and the left half controls the right side of your body. The left half of your brain is good at thinking and working things out, talking, and doing maths and other complicated tasks. The right half helps you to identify objects and recognise faces. It's good at helping you do creative things such as painting and playing music.

The left half of your brain helps you to do practical tasks such as maths.

$$1 \times 1 = 1 \quad 2 \times 4 = 8$$
$$2 \times$$

Working together

The two halves work together.
For example, when your eyes see
a house, the right half identifies
the picture as a house. The left half
looks through your memories, to see
if you know something about
the house, for example where it is
or who lives in it.

The right half of your brain helps you to do creative tasks such as art.

Organisational centre

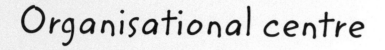

Your brain's organisational centre is in your forebrain too, right at the front of your brain under your forehead.

It is here that your brain does all its planning. For example, you use your organisational centre to work out the order in which to do something, such as getting dressed in the morning or baking a cake. Your problem-solving centre is here as well. You use it a lot – for example, to work out how to build something or solve a puzzle.

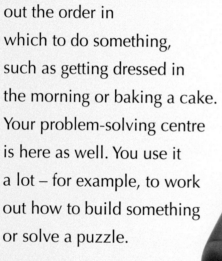

Emotions

Emotions are feelings, for example,
being sad, happy, angry or hungry.
Your forebrain helps you
to control your emotions.
When you feel angry, it stops
you from hitting somebody.
When you feel hungry,
it makes you want to
eat something.

Using language

Language is very important in our daily lives. You use language to talk to your family and friends, to share ideas with them, and to read and write. You use words to describe your thoughts and feelings. Language helps everybody to work together.

Your language centre is found in the left half of your forebrain. It's good at organisation. Your brain has to listen to sounds and produce sounds. It puts sounds in the right order so that people can understand what you're saying.

New languages

Some people find it easy to learn a new language, but others struggle. Scientists have found that people who are good at languages have a larger language centre.

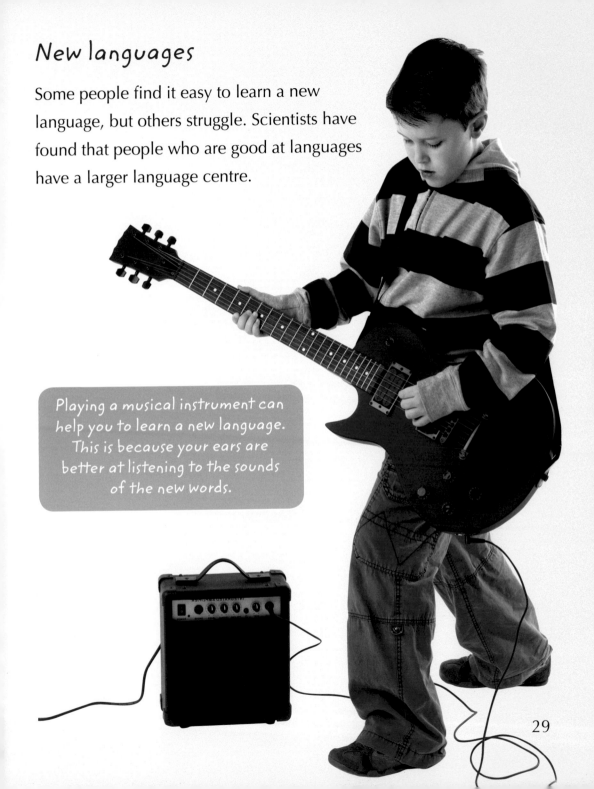

Playing a musical instrument can help you to learn a new language. This is because your ears are better at listening to the sounds of the new words.

Memories

You have all sorts of memories. There are memories of things you've seen, sounds you've heard, smells you've sniffed, books you've read and places you've visited. Your memories are stored in your forebrain so that you can recall them again in the future.

Short- and long-term memories

Some memories are stored in your short-term memory store for a few minutes. These are things like a telephone number that you are about to use, or numbers for a maths problem. Only a few things are stored in your short-term memory at a time.

Useful memories are stored in your long-term memory, where they may stay for a lifetime – for example, memories of how to ride a bike, or of important events like holidays or birthday parties. These memories are a bit like files stored on a computer. However, our brains can't remember everything, unlike a computer!

Automatic control

There are many things taking place in
your body that you have no control over.
These are the **automatic** functions that your
brain controls without you having to do anything.
Your hindbrain is involved with these essential processes;
for example, the beating of your heart, breathing and the
digesting of your food have to go on all the time. These
processes happen automatically as you have lots of other things to
think about.

Heart and lungs

Your hindbrain controls how quickly your heart is beating and makes sure that blood is pumping around your body.
It makes you breathe too. You can control your breathing if you think about it.
But once you're busy doing something else, your hindbrain takes over.
It also controls things like coughing, sneezing and swallowing.

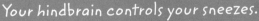
Your hindbrain controls your sneezes.

Body temperature

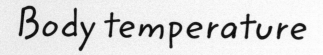

Your brain controls your body temperature too. It knows that your body temperature should be kept at about 37 degrees centigrade.

> The part of your brain that controls your body temperature is called the hypothalamus.

> Your brain controls your body temperature.

Controlling your temperature

It's important that you don't get too hot or too cold. Your brain receives information about your body temperature from all over your body. If your body temperature falls, your brain starts processes to warm you up. You start **shivering** and this helps to make you warm again. If you're too hot, your brain tells your body to sweat. When you sweat, your skin produces a watery liquid which **evaporates** into the air. This helps to cool you down.

Keeping your balance

Your brain makes sure you can stand up and walk without falling over. This is called co-ordination and your co-ordination centre is found in the hindbrain. The hindbrain works closely with your forebrain, which stores all the information from your senses.

Balancing act

When you want to stand up, your forebrain sends information about your surroundings to your hindbrain – for example, where you're sitting and what's in front of you. Then your hindbrain sends messages to the muscles in your legs, telling them to push your body up and move your legs forwards. The muscles have to be moved in the right order, otherwise you fall over!

Information from the ears

You use information from your ears too. Your ears can sense the position of your head. Every time you move your head, messages race along nerves to your brain. This means you know if you're bending over or standing up straight.

While you sleep

Your brain never switches off, even when you're sleeping. When you sleep, your body rests and repairs itself, while your brain files away the day's memories and also dreams.

Brain cycles

When you sleep, your brain goes through three types of sleep – light sleep, deep sleep and one called REM, which stands for rapid eye movements. At first, you drift into light sleep. It's easy to wake someone during light sleep. When you're in deep sleep you breathe slowly and your brain is not very active. Your body repairs itself and prepares for the day ahead.

Every night you spend up to two hours dreaming.

It's difficult to wake someone when they're in deep sleep. During REM sleep your eyes flutter and move in all directions, while your eyelids are closed. Your brain is busy, filing away important memories and deleting others. You dream during REM, too.

Dreams and nightmares

A dream is a mixture of lots of strange things. Sometimes dreams are
linked to things that have happened to us, sometimes they're not.
If you wake up while you're dreaming, you may remember your dream.
Nightmares are scary thoughts and images that occur during deep sleep.
A common nightmare is being chased by a person or animal.
Sometimes the nightmare is so real that you wake up feeling very scared.

A healthy brain

Your brain works hard every day of your life,
so it's important to look after it.

Protecting your brain

Your brain can be injured in accidents and bangs to the head.
Your skull does a good job of protecting it, but sometimes you need
extra protection. If you cycle or ride a horse, or go climbing or
skateboarding, you have to
wear a safety helmet to
protect your head in case
you have an accident.

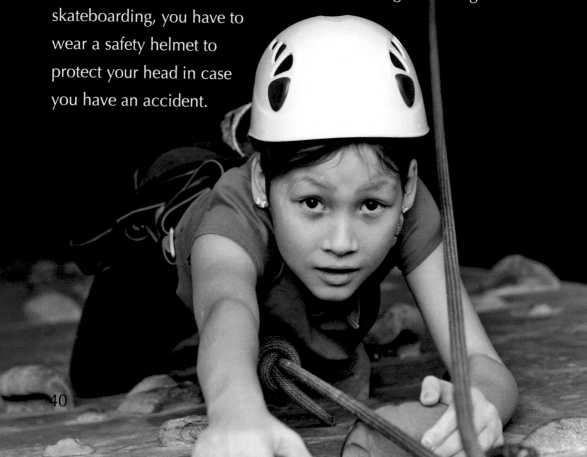

Headaches

Headaches are very common and you've probably had
a headache already. A headache is when you feel pain inside
your head. The brain itself can't feel any pain, so the pain comes from
around your brain. There are many causes of a headache,
but the most common is caused by muscles in your head and neck.
The muscles tighten and you feel them squeezing your head and this
causes the pain.

Looking after your brain

If you want a healthy brain, you need to have a fit and healthy body. You need to use your brain every day – for example, learning something new or doing a puzzle. A good night's sleep helps your brain to concentrate. If you're unfit or overweight and don't use your brain every day, your brain may not work so well.

Playing games keeps your brain active.

Getting older

As you get older, your brain cells start to die and aren't replaced. When you have fewer brain cells, your memories aren't so clear, especially your short-term memories. You have to exercise your brain to keep it working properly – for example, by doing crosswords, reading books and playing musical instruments.

Glossary

automatic   happening without you having to think of it

balance   the ability to stand upright and steady

blood vessels   small tubes that carry your blood around your body

digestion   when your food is broken down into very small parts in your stomach

evaporates   changes from a liquid to a gas, because of heat

memory   the ability to remember things that have happened

oxygen   the part of the air that you breathe which keeps you alive

recognises   knows something because it's been seen before

senses   sight, hearing, touch, smell and taste, which all pass information to your brain from the outside world

shivering   shaking uncontrollably

stringy   long and thin, like a piece of string

Index

Things your brain does every day

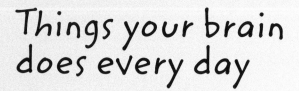

You plan and organise from here.

You feel temperature from here.

Your emotions are controlled here.

You learn languages here.

Your automatic functions and balance are controlled here.

You store your memories here.

Ideas for reading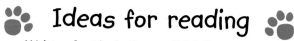

Written by Linda Pagett B.Ed (hons), M.Ed
Lecturer and Educational Consultant

Learning objectives: identify and make notes of the main sections of text; use some drama strategies to explore issues; use knowledge of organisational features to find information; summarise information from a text

Curriculum links: Science

Interest words: automatic, backbone, balance, blood vessels, cells, digestion, evaporates, forebrain, hemispheres, hindbrain, memory, midbrain, oxygen, recognises, senses, shivering, skull, spinal cord, stringy, synapse

Resources: whiteboard, modelling clay, paint

Getting started

This book can be read over two or more reading sessions.

- Introduce the book by reading the blurb and ask the children to predict what sort of book this is and what they think they'll learn from it.

- Invite all the children to discuss anything they already know about the human brain. Make a list on the whiteboard, then discuss. Note what they would like to learn through reading the book.

- Using the contents page, allot different chapters to different children.

Reading and responding

- Direct children to read quietly, noting any new information to add to the chart and any tricky words they are unsure of.

- On pp26–34, ensure that the children understand that the blue spots on the brain diagrams refer to the part of the brain that is being talked about in the text.

- Support weaker readers as they read, prompting and praising where necessary, and direct early finishers to browse unread chapters, noting what attracts their attention.